MOVE!

Foreword

Every day, Reuters photojournalists move with the story to capture the world in action.

A canoeist gasps as he steers through chaotic water rapids. A prisoner reaches out through rigid cell bars. Cardinals' elaborate garments billow in a gust of wind. A policeman fires a teargas canister at protestors. War refugees pause in a moment of embrace. These are split seconds of exceptional action photographs.

Move! is a powerful high-speed photographic journey. From the most recognised images to unexpected others, this special selection illustrates the momentum that reverberates through so many aspects of life.

Monique Villa and Tom Szlukovenyi

Akram Saleh
A man retrieves his luggage from the scene of a bomb attack at Baghdad's Sheheen hotel, January 2004.

Vladimir Pirogov
Kyrgyz policemen drag away an opposition protester in Bishkek,
November 2002.

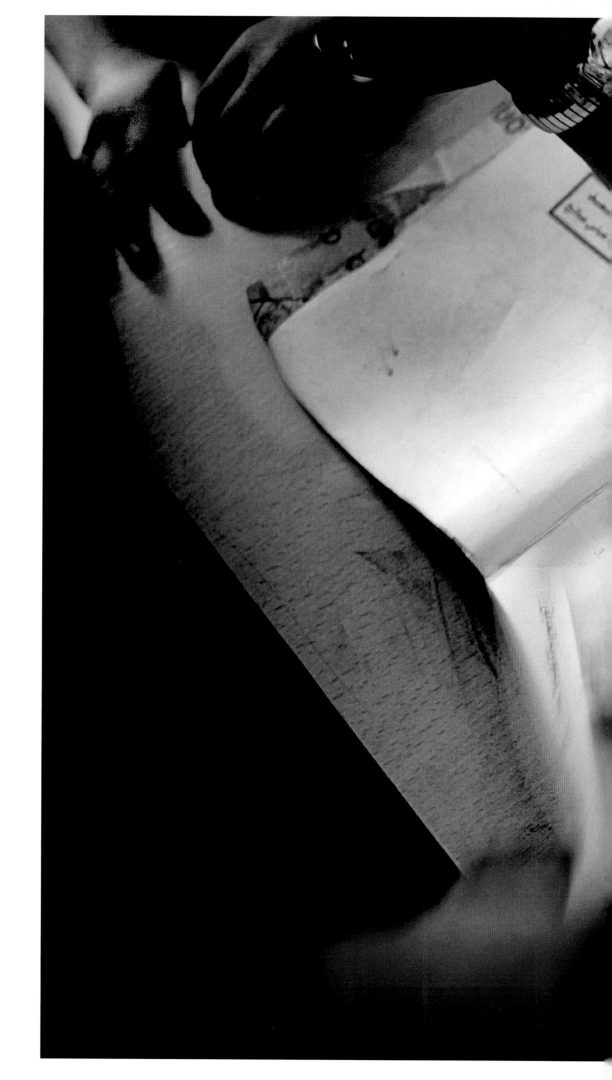

Kieran Doherty

A teacher removes a portrait of former president Saddam
Hussein from a school textbook, May 2003.

Max Rossi
Cardinals' cassocks are blown by a gust of wind as they arrive for the funeral mass of Pope John Paul II at St. Peter's Basilica, April 2005.

Koen van Weel

A competitor of a mud race climbs out of one of 22 ditches along the 3km course in meadow lands near Monnickendam, Netherlands, June 2005.

Goran Tomasevic
A Palestinian woman throws olives in the air as she works in the
West Bank village of Deir Al-Hatab, October 2004.

Marc Serota
A man seeks shelter in a hotel car park as Hurricane Ivan moves
into Pensacola, Florida, September 2004.

Jacky Naegelen

Cyclists pass in front of a chemical plant during the 150.5 km first
stage of the Tour of Qatar cycling race in Doha, February 2004.

Kai Pfaffenbach
Romania's Marius Urzica competes on the pommel horse during
the Gymnastics World Cup in Stuttgart, November 2004.

Max Rossi
Canadian Jeff Pain speeds down the track on his sled during the
men's Skeleton World Cup in Cesana Pariol, January 2005.

Philippe Wojazer
Cabaret dancers leave the stage during a performance of the
show 'Bonheur' at the Lido in Paris, February 2005.

Tony Gentile
Italian commuters stroll in front of a train at Termini station in
Rome, July 2004.

Yves Herman
Revellers dance during the 'Gay and Lesbian Pride' rally in
Brussels, May 2005.

Adrees Latif
Thai contestants practice backstage at the annual Miss Tiffany's
Universe 2005 transvestite contest in Pattaya, May 2005.

Ina Fassbender

A girl dressed as Santa Claus starts a running competition at the opening of the Christmas market in Düsseldorf, November 2004.

Marcelo del Pozo

A bull prepares to charge during a bullfight in the Maestranza bullring in Seville, April 2004.

Caren Firouz
'Who Knows Lilly', ridden by Argentina's Frederico Sztyrle,
clears a jump during a qualifying round of the show jumping
competition at the Athens Olympic Games, August 2004.

Gleb Garanich
Ukrainian National Guard cadets march through Kiev during a military parade, August 2004.

Damir Sagolj
A young man sits on top of a street light, in front of the United Nations building, waving a Lebanese flag during a pro-Syrian rally in central Beirut, March 2005.

Damir Sagolj

A man jumps off the newly rebuilt arch of Stari Most during
the traditional diving competition in the Bosnian town of Mostar,
July 2004.

Arko Datta
Indian laundrymen known as 'dhobis' wash clothes in open air
laundries in Bombay, September 2004.

Mohsin Raza
A Pakistani devotee dances at the shrine of Muslim saint Madhu
Shah Lal Hussain in Lahore, March 2005.

Jorge Silva
A reveller dances during Carnival in Port of Spain's Queen's Park
Savannah in Trinidad, February 2005.

Albert Gea

Ukraine's Yana Klochkova competes in the 200 metre individual medley at the World Swimming Championships in Barcelona, July 2003.

Damir Sagolj
France's Nicolas Peschier makes his way down the slalom course
in a men's canoe single heat at the Athens Olympic Games,
August 2004.

Howard Burditt
A Zambian man somersaults into a pool at the edge of the 110 metre high Victoria Falls on the Zambezi river between Zambia and Zimbabwe, October 2004.

Wolfgang Rattay
Iran's Hossein Rezazadeh prays as he celebrates his gold medal
in the men's super-heavyweight weightlifting event at the Athens
Olympic Games, August 2004.

Toru Hanai
Japanese sumo wrestler Kotomitsuki (right) heaves Tochinonada
onto the sumo ring at the New Year Grand Sumo tournament in
Tokyo, January 2005.

Alessandro Bianchi

A model wears a creation from the Trend les Copains Spring/Summer 2004 collection at Milan fashion week, October 2003.

Yannis Behrakis

A member of the Ukrainian synchronised swimming team performs a free routine during an Olympic Games qualification tournament in Athens, April 2004.

Chaiwat Subprasom
A Thai man rides his ox in the 133rd annual Buffalo Racing festival in the province of Chon Buri, October 2004.

Radu Sigheti
A Kenyan jockey competes in an ostrich race during celebrations marking 100 years of horse racing in Nairobi, October 2004.

Shamil Zhumatov
A Kazakh hunter rides with an eagle during a traditional hunting contest near the town of Taldykorgan, some 270 miles north of Almaty, January 2004.

Stoyan Nenov
A dog spins in the air from a twisted rope over a pool, during an annual ritual near the village of Brodilovo in Bulgaria, March 2005.

John Gress
Atlanta Hawks guard Josh Smith leaps over Denver Nuggets forward Kenyon Martin during the slam dunk competition at the 2005 NBA All-Star Saturday Night in Colorado, February 2005.

Marcelo del Pozo
Spanish matador Dávila Miura prepares to perform a pass, as
the shadow of the bull is cast onto the muleta during a bullfight
in the Maestranza bullring in Seville, April 2003.

Gustau Nacarino
Spanish flamenco dancer Sara Baras performs 'Choreography
Dreams' during the Millennium Barcelona festival at the Palau
de la Música, January 2005.

Jerry Lampen
Members of the Dutch Royal Guard rehearse for the Dutch 2005 budget presentation at Scheveningen, September 2004.

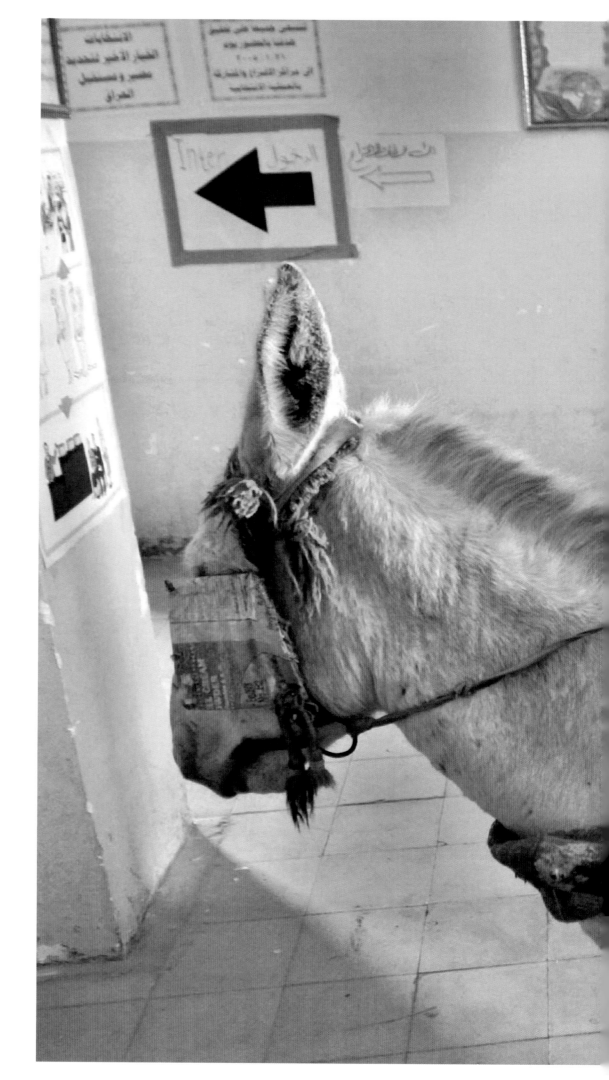

Atef Hassan

An Iraqi police officer carries out a security check of a donkey, pulling a disabled man on a cart, before allowing it to enter a polling station in Basra, January 2005.

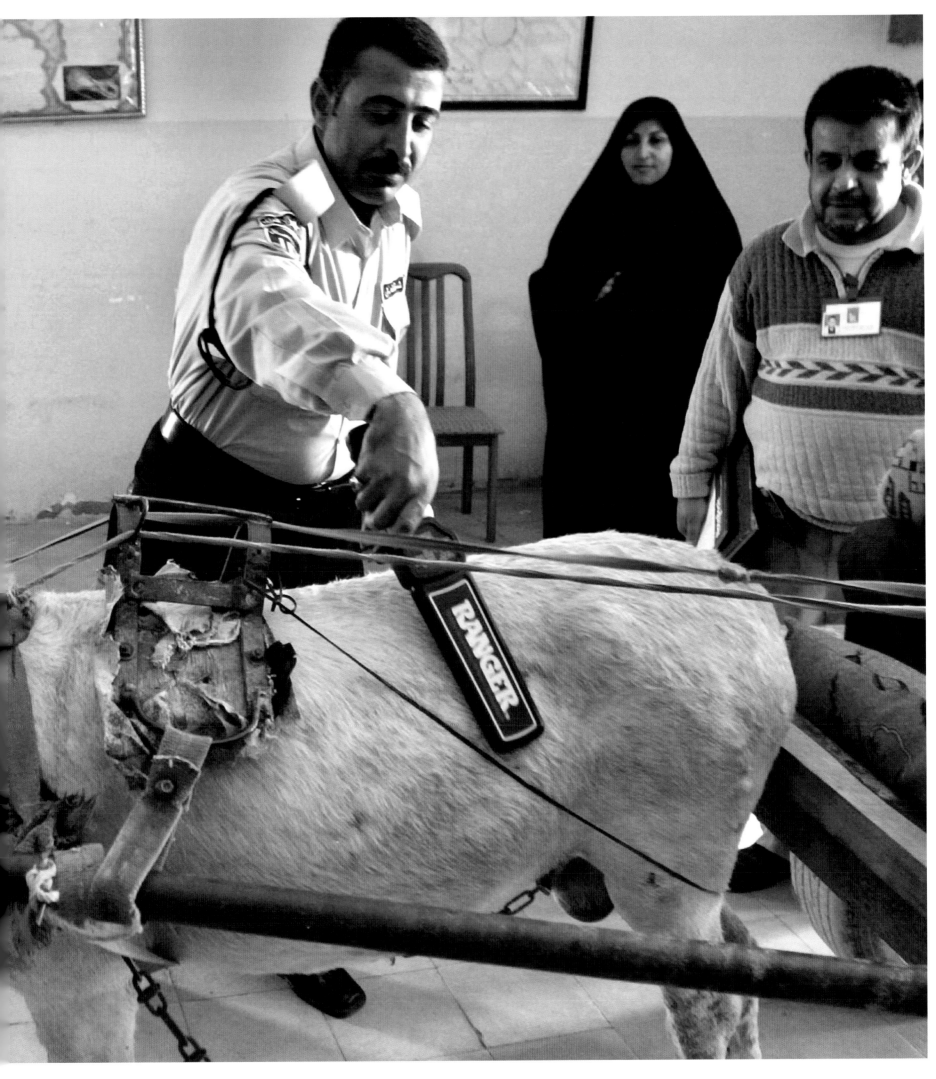

Andrea Comas
Dancers perform during a rehearsal at the Pradillo theatre in
Madrid, April 2005.

Srdjan Zivulovic
A member of the Slovenian army rides a Lipizaner at a newly
established horse unit in Lipica, May 2005.

Jacky Naegelen
A runner makes his way through litter scattered over the
Champs-Elysees during the start of the 26th Paris Marathon,
April 2002.

Dani Cardona
A woman watches cyclists pass through the village of Muro
during the Mallorca Challenge race, February 2005.

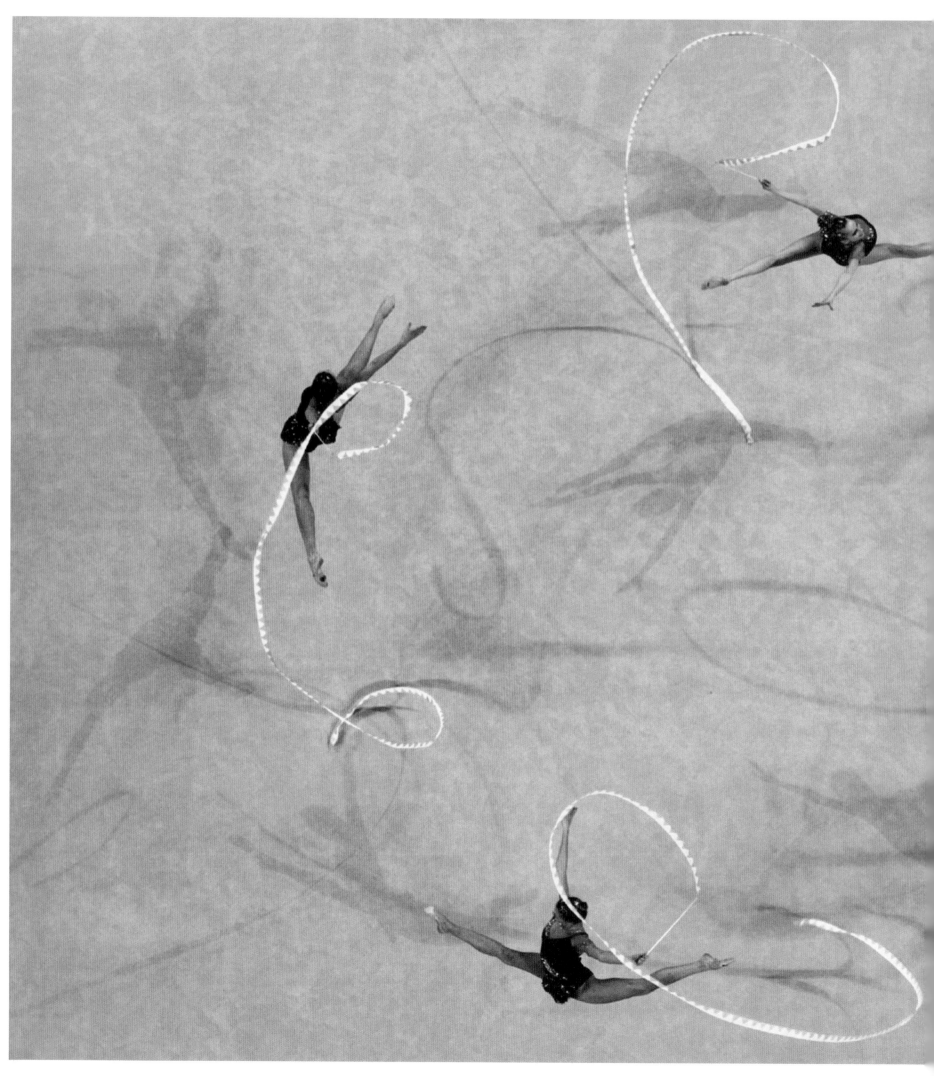

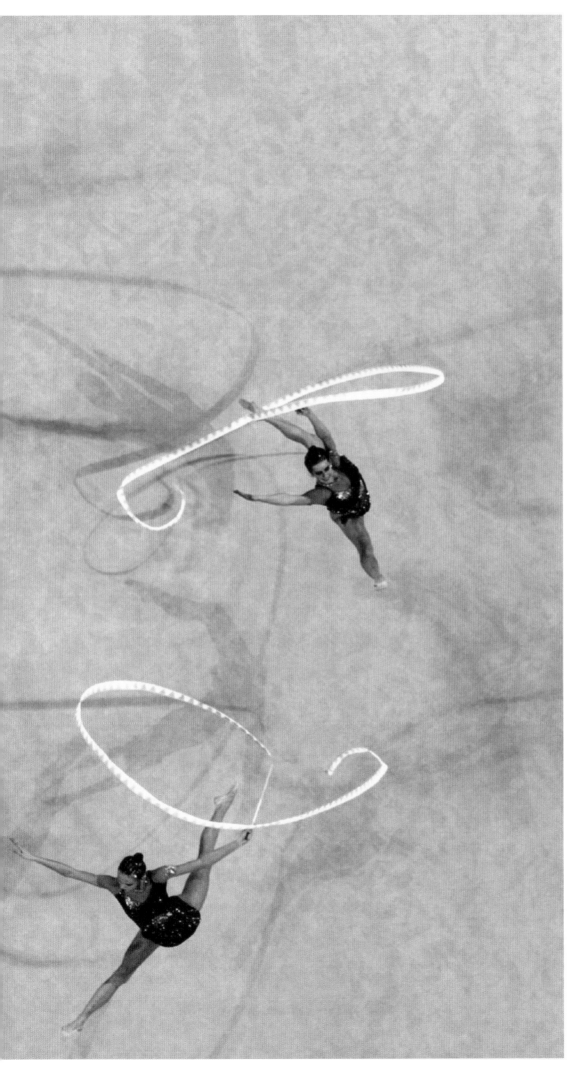

John Kolesidis
Polish athletes compete in the rhythmic gymnastics ribbon event during tests for the Athens Olympic Games, March 2004.

Bobby Yip
Protesters stage a pro-democracy march on the seventh
anniversary of Hong Kong's handover to China, July 2004.

Vasily Fedosenko
Olga Kapranova of Russia performs with a ball during the
Rhythmic Gymnastics Grand Prix in Minsk, May 2004.

Stephen Hird
Justin Hawkins, lead singer of British rock band 'The Darkness' performs on stage at the Brit Awards 2004 in London, February 2004.

Gary Hershorn
In a composite photograph, the moon is seen in transition, from left to right, from a full state to a state of full lunar eclipse in the evening sky over Washington, October 2004.

Carlos Barria
Spectators watch a fashion show by Colombian designer Liliana
Fierro during Miami fashion week, May 2005.

David Gray
Trapeze artist Ali Weaver swings high in the Circus Oz 'Big Top' during a performance in Sydney, December 2004.

Viktor Korotayev
Performers from the Argentine 'De La Guarda' theatre company perform in Moscow, January 2005.

Kieran Doherty
Russia and Germany fight for the gold medal in the women's fencing team epee at the Athens 2004 Olympic Games, August 2004.

Dima Korotayev
Italians Federica Faiella and Massimo Scali perform at the figure skating Grand Prix of Russia in Moscow, November 2004.

Dylan Martinez
A Venetian dressed in traditional costume strolls through
St. Mark's Square as the sun sets on the Venice Carnival,
February 2004.

Laszlo Balogh
A bather relaxes in the famous Szechenyi thermal spring baths
in Hungary, October 2003.

Bruno Domingos
Brazilian firemen try in vain to save a stranded humpback whale for the third consecutive day on Jurujuba beach in Rio de Janeiro, August 2004.

Marcelo del Pozo
Australia's Natalie Cook falls during a beach volleyball match at
the Athens 2004 Olympic Games, August 2004.

Heinz-Peter Bader
Georg Späth of Germany soars through the air during the Ski
Jumping World Championships in Planica, February 2004.

Alexander Demianchuk

A woman crosses Dvortsovaya Square in central St. Petersburg during a snowstorm, November 2004.

Rick Fowler
Guests ride 'Soarin', a new attraction at the EPCOT Center,
during Disney's 50th anniversary celebration in Lake Buena
Vista, Florida, May 2005.

Arko Datta
A Sri Lankan man holds an umbrella as he cycles under overcast skies in Kalmunai, days after the bay was hit by the Asian tsunami, January 2005.

Mike Hutchings
Young, aspiring footballers train in Johannesburg, South Africa,
April 2004.

Mike Hutchings
South African rugby player Ashwin Willemse takes a high ball
during a training session in Brisbane, October 2003.

Oleg Popov
A Bulgarian woman dances on smouldering embers during an
ancient ritual in the village of Bulgari, June 2003.

Simon Baker
South Africa's Natal Sharks Craig Davidson looks up at the
referee to see his match winning try confirmed during a Super
12 rugby clash against New Zealand's Otago Highlanders in
Dunedin, March 2004.

Damir Sagolj
Spain's Sergio Garcia celebrates scoring against Bosnia during
the Under-21 European Championship 2006 qualifier in Sarajevo,
September 2004.

China Newsphoto
A 13-year-old Chinese girl of Miao ethnicity walks on knife points
during the traditional ethnic sports games in Guiyang, May 2005.

Bob Strong
A man looks at his wife and baby as he is searched by U.S. Army soldiers from the 10th Mountain Division at a traffic checkpoint in Baghdad, March 2005.

Arko Datta

An Indian woman breaks down outside a hospital ward while her eight-year-old son undergoes treatment for serious burns from a school fire in Kumbakonam, July 2004.

Adeel Halim
An Indian boy swims in a muddy pool of water during hot
weather in Bombay, April 2005.

Fabrizio Bensch
Students dance to the choreography of Maurice Ravel's ballet
'Daphnis and Chloé' during a dress rehearsal for a cultural youth
project in Berlin, February 2004.

David Gray
Boys crouch behind a sea-pool wall as they play in the massive
surf at Sydney's Narrabeen beach, February 2004.

Arko Datta
Indian children play in waves splashing onto the waterfront
during hot weather in Bombay, June 2004.

Jessica Rinaldi
Light and leaves are reflected in a waterfall along the Blackberry river in Connecticut, October 2004.

Bazuki Muhammad
A trevally chases fusiliers near Malaysia's Lankayan island in the Sulu-Sulawesi Marine Ecoregion, January 2004.

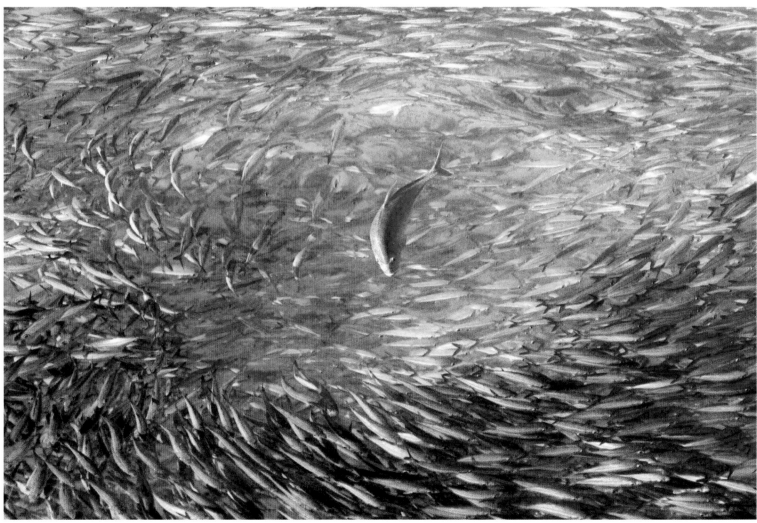

David Gray
A passenger plane flies past storm clouds after taking-off from
Sydney Airport, November 2004.

Philippe Laurenson
Dense smoke rises into the sky after the wind drove flames
through 200 hectares of forest, near the district of l'Estaque in
Marseille, July 2004.

Mohammad Shahidullah

A Bangladeshi shop owner cries as fire destroys a market in Dhaka, November 2004.

Goran Tomasevic

A Palestinian protester lies on the ground as Israeli border police try to arrest him during a demonstration against the construction of Israel's security barrier in the West Bank village of Biddu, April 2004.

Eduard Kornienko
A man carries an injured boy from a school seized by heavily armed men and women in Beslan near Chechnya, September 2004.

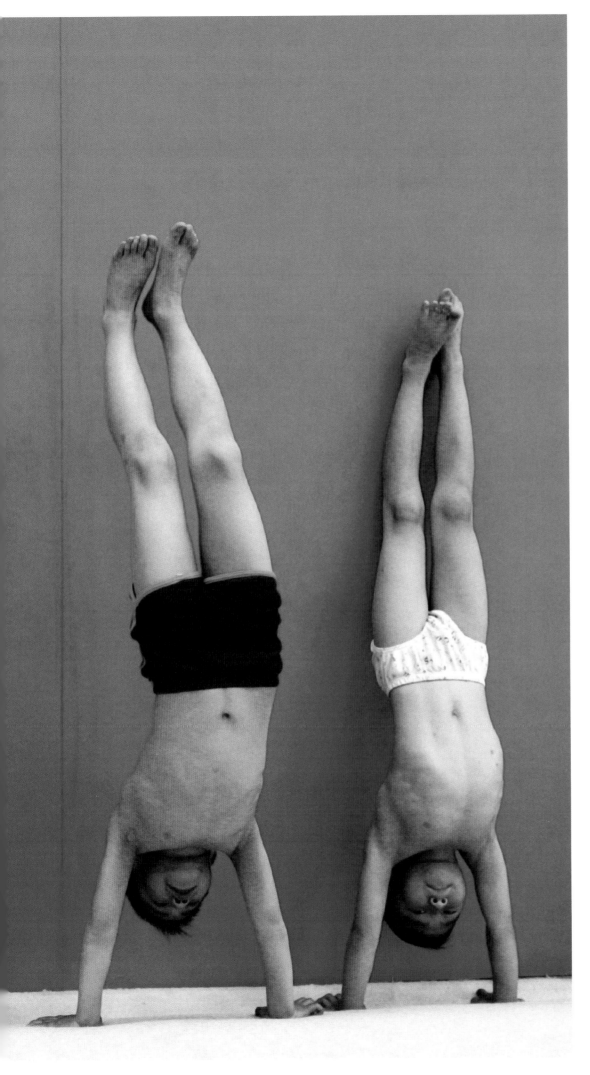

Reinhard Krause
Young Chinese athletes perform handstands in a gymnastic hall at the Beijing Shihahai Sports School, December 2004.

Guang Niu
A Chinese shoe saleswoman waits for customers at a shopping
centre in Beijing, May 2004.

Damir Sagolj
An athlete runs past a statue on the last lap of the men's marathon at the Athens Olympic Games, August 2004.

David Gray
Canadian swimmer Morgan Knabe rests on the swimming pool deck during a morning training session in Athens, August 2004.

Francois Lenoir
Kenya's Daniel Komen runs in the men's 1500 metres event at the Flanders international indoor athletic meeting in Ghent, February 2005.

David Gray
Estonian runner Erki Nool's shoes are left on the track after the men's 1500 metres event of the decathlon at the Athens Olympic Games, August 2004.

Jose Manuel Ribeiro
An athlete warms up during a training session for the IAAF World Indoor Athletics championships in Lisbon, March 2001.

Claro Cortes IV
A member of the Chinese paramilitary People's Armed Police
yawns during a military drill in Beijing, November 2004.

Yannis Behrakis
A pilgrim crawls towards the Church of Virgin Mary during Easter
eve celebrations on the Greek Island of Tinos, April 2004.

Kimo Akal
An Iraqi army soldier crawls outside a polling station to cast
his vote during his country's national elections in Baghdad,
January 2005.

Darren Whiteside
Police scuffle with students protesting against government fuel price hikes outside the parliament in Jakarta, March 2005.

You Sung-Ho
Former South Korean spy soldiers, trained to infiltrate North Korea, are blocked by riot policemen while they try to enter the Japanese embassy at a rally in Seoul, February 2005.

Sergei Vasiliev
Belarussian soldiers dressed in Red Army uniforms march during a military parade in Minsk marking the 60th anniversary of the Soviet victory over Nazism, May 2005.

Vasily Fedosenko
A Ukrainian woman places carnations into the shields of anti-riot policemen outside the presidential office in Kiev, November 2004.

Damir Sagolj
Fighting bulls approach a barrier during the 7th bull run of the
San Fermin festival in Pamplona, July 2003.

Mark Wallheiser
A woman prays for Terri Schiavo, who had been in a persistent vegetative state since 1990, in front of the Florida governor's mansion during a candlelight vigil in Tallahassee, March 2005.

Jayanta Shaw
An Indian girl waves from inside a plane as she leaves Campbell Bay after a tsunami hit the remote Andaman and Nicobar island chain, December 2004.

Damir Sagolj

An Iraqi detainee gestures towards U.S. soldiers through the bars of his cell at Abu Ghraib prison outside Baghdad, May 2004.

Bobby Yip
A snake retreats into a drawer in a store in Hong Kong selling
snake soup, which is considered to be a health-giving delicacy,
January 2004.

Reinhard Krause

A Chinese construction worker makes final touches to a newly
built skyscraper in Beijing's financial district, December 2004.

Richard Chung
A pedestrian wades through a flooded street in the Taiwanese,
typhoon-hit town of Shangchung, August 2004.

ɹuhaib Salem

 Palestinian boy jumps through a ring of fire in front of U.S. and
 raeli flags during an Islamic Jihad movement anti-Israel rally in
 aza, April 2005.

Goran Tomasevic
An Israeli border policeman fires a teargas canister during a
Palestinian protest against the construction of the Israeli security
barrier in the West Bank village of Az-Zawiya, June 2004.

Mahfouz Abu Turk

A Palestinian man performs a somersault next to the Israeli West Bank security barrier near the village of Abu Dis, March 2004.

Jeff J Mitchell
A young girl puts her fingers in her ears as Britain's Prime Minister
Tony Blair addresses the spring Labour Party conference in
Gateshead, February 2005.

Goran Tomasevic
A Palestinian man reacts after using a slingshot to throw a stone at Israeli border policemen at the construction site of Israel's security barrier near the West Bank village of Beit Surik, March 2005.

arry Downing

J.S. President George W. Bush is chased by a cicada as he walks
p the steps to Air Force One at Andrews Air Force Base in
irginia, May 2004.

Reinhard Krause

Palestinian youths run to escape from Israeli soldiers firing teargas
as another youth crawls in the opposite direction during clashes in
the southern Gaza town of Khan Younis, October 2000.

Desmond Boylan

An Afghan security guard plays with a dog on a hill overlooking Kabul, September 2004.

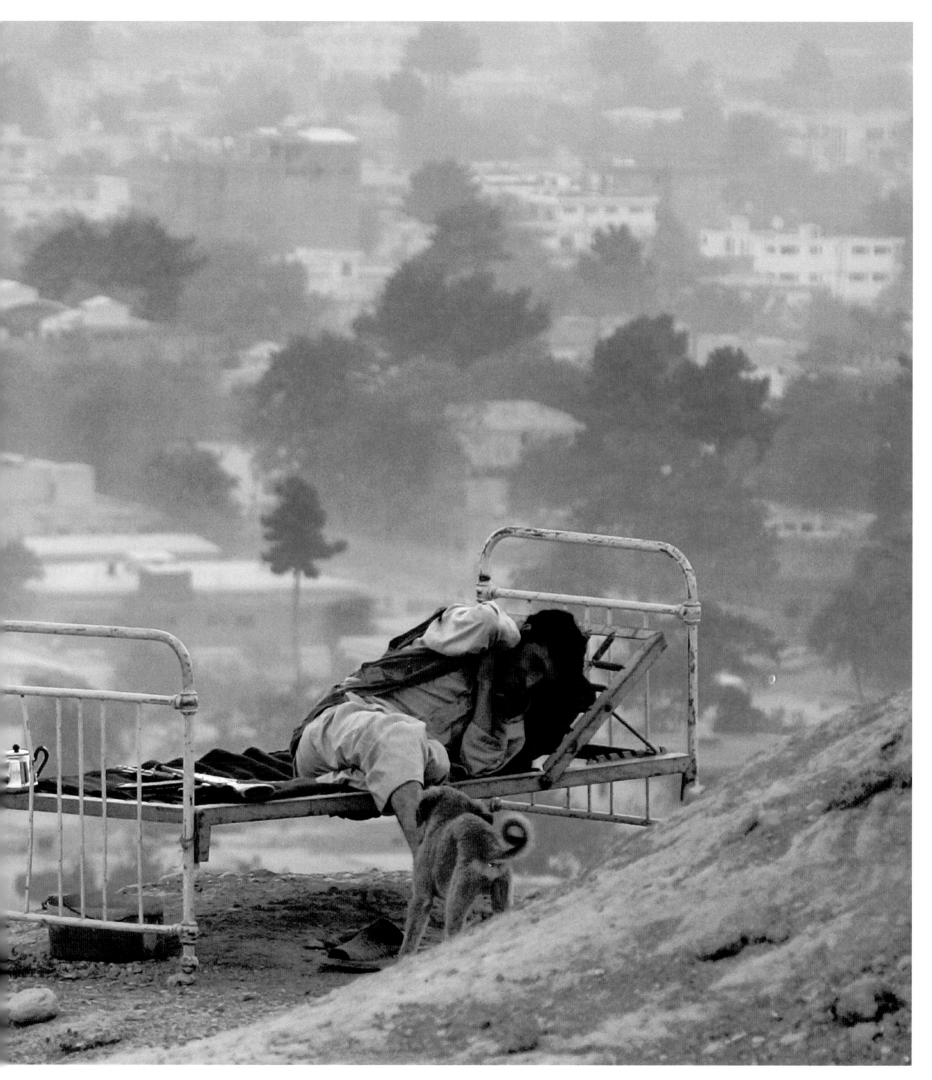

Photographers

Kimo Akal

Born in Baghdad, Iraq in 1975. Kimo worked as a cameraman for Iraqi TV before joining Reuters in 2004.

Heinz-Peter Bader

Born in Vienna, Austria in 1966. Heinz-Peter has worked for Reuters since March 1992.

Simon Baker

Born in Matamata, New Zealand in 1966. Simon has been a photojournalist for over 20 years, based in New Zealand. He has covered events in the UK, Australia, Pacific and New Zealand as a Reuters freelancer for approximately 15 years.

Laszlo Balogh

Born in Budapest, Hungary in 1958. Laszlo joined Reuters in 1990 and is now Hungary Chief Photographer.

Carlos Barria

Born in Bariloche, Argentina in 1979. Started with Reuters as a freelance photographer based in Buenos Aires in 2000. In 2001, he won the 1st prize in the General News Singles category of the World Press Photo awards for his work on the riots during the Argentine crisis. After working in Chile, he is now based in Miami for Reuters.

Yannis Behrakis

Born in Athens, Greece in 1960. Yannis began working for Reuters in 1987 and is now Greece Chief Photographer. Over the past 15 years, he has covered a variety of events including the funeral of Ayatollah Khomeini in Iran, changes in Eastern Europe and the Balkans, conflicts in Croatia, Bosnia and Kosovo, wars in Chechnya, Sierra Leone, Somalia, Afghanistan and the Gulf. Among several prestigious awards he has been named six times News Photographer of the Year by the Greek National Fuji Awards.

Fabrizio Bensch

Born in Berlin, Germany in 1969. Fabrizio has been working for Reuters since 1992 based in Berlin and has travelled the world covering both news and sports stories.

Alessandro Bianchi

Born in Rome, Italy in 1967. Alessandro began freelancing for national newspapers and magazines in 1992. He joined ANSA in 1995 and Reuters in 2003.

Desmond Boylan

Born in London, UK in 1964. Desmond joined Reuters in Madrid in 1992 and is now India Chief Photographer, based in Delhi. He has covered major news, feature and sport events around the world and conflicts in the Middle East, Africa and the Balkans.

Howard Burditt

Born in Harare, Zimbabwe in 1958. Howard joined Reuters as a southern African freelancer in 1987.

Dani Cardona

Born in Palma de Mallorca, Spain, in 1971. Dani started his career in 1997 and joined Reuters as a freelancer based in Mallorca.

Richard Chung

Born in Taipei, Taiwan in 1969. Richard worked for local newspapers before joining Reuters in 2002.

Andrea Comas

Born in Konstanz, Germany in 1972. Andrea has worked for Reuters since 1999, based in Madrid. She has covered stories in the Gaza Strip and Iraq and covered the earthquake in Morocco and the Madrid bombings in 2004.

Claro Cortes IV

Born in Manila, Philippines in 1960. Claro works for the Reuters Shanghai bureau in China. He was the first recipient of the Willie Vicoy-Reuter Fellowship at the University of Missouri in Columbia in 1987.

Arko Datta

Born in Delhi, India in 1969. Arko worked for two Indian national dailies and Agence France-Presse before joining Reuters in 2001. He has covered stories in Iraq, Afghanistan, Kashmir and the India-Pakistan border. Datta won the prestigious World Press Photo award in 2005 for a picture of a grieving woman after the tsunami.

Alexander Demianchuk

Born in Kovel, West Ukraine, in 1959. After working for Russian and local St. Petersburg newspapers he joined Reuters in 1991, based in St. Petersburg. Alexander has covered the wars in Chechnya and Iraq in addition to other major news events.

Kieran Doherty

Born in Dover, England in 1968. Kieran has worked for Reuters since 1993. Based in London, he has covered a variety of national and international stories, including the Iraq conflict, 60th anniversary of the D-Day landings and the Asian tsunami.

Bruno Domingos

Born in Rio de Janeiro, Brazil in 1977. Bruno started his career in 1999 at the Jornal Dos Sports daily and then Lance sports newspaper. He joined Reuters in 2003 as a freelancer, based in Rio de Janeiro.

Ina Fassbender

Born in Schleiden, Germany in 1965. Ina started working freelance as a sports photographer in 1994 for newspapers, magazines and television and began working for Reuters in 1998.

Vasily Fedosenko

Born in Bobrujsk, Belarus in 1960. Vasily started with Reuters as a freelancer based in Belarus' capital Minsk in 1997 and became a staff photographer in 2000.

Caren Firouz

Born in Shiraz, Iran in 1962. Firouz joined Reuters in Iran in 1998 and is now the Tehran bureau photo editor and photographer outside Iran. He has covered the first Gulf War and the Kurdish uprising in northern Iraq. In Africa, he covered the arrival of U.S. forces in Somalia and elections in Kenya.

Rick Fowler

Born in Bagdad, Arizona, USA in 1968. He has worked for Reuters since 1985.

Gleb Garanich

Born on Sakhalin Island, Russia in 1969. Gleb joined Reuters in 1995, based in Kiev.

Albert Gea

Born in Barcelona in 1977. Albert worked for motorcycle magazine Piloto before joining Reuters as a freelancer in July 2000.

Tony Gentile

Born in Palermo, Italy in 1964. Tony began working as a Reuters freelancer in 1992 before joining the team in Rome.

David Gray

Born in Sydney, Australia in 1971. David was a sports photographer at The Australian in 1993 before joining Reuters in 1996. He is now Australia Chief Photographer. David has covered events in Australia, Papua New Guinea and New Zealand, as well as political unrest in Indonesia and East Timor. He has won numerous awards, most recently winning Gold in the Features category at Publish Asia 2005.

John Gress

Born in Oregon City, Oregon. John worked for the Associated Press from 1996 and joined Reuters in 2003 in Chicago.

Adeel Halim

Born in Bombay, India in 1979. Adeel started working for Reuters in 2005.

Toru Hanai

Born in Tokyo, Japan in 1973. Toru joined Reuters in 2005 after working nine years for a Japanese sports newspaper in Tokyo.

Atef Hassan

Born in Basra, Iraq in 1976. Atef began working for Reuters in 2003.

Yves Herman

Born in Brussels, Belgium in 1968. Yves joined Reuters in 1997.

Gary Hershorn

Born in Ontario, Canada in 1958. Gary joined Reuters as Canada Chief Photographer and then transferred to Washington in 1990. He is now Chief Photographer for the Americas. Gary has won numerous prizes, including most recently first place for Sports at the White House Press Photographers' Association contest.

Stephen Hird
Born in England in 1969. Stephen worked for the Daily Telegraph from 1997 before joining Reuters in 2000.

Pierre Holtz
Born in France in 1971. Since January 2004 Pierre has been based in Dakar, Senegal, from where he regularly works for the United Nations news agency IRIN, Reuters and Spiegel. Pierre won second prize in the Nature category at the World Press Photo competition in 2005.

Mike Hutchings
Born in London, UK in 1963. Mike started working for Reuters in 1991 as a freelancer and covered the historic first democratic elections that brought Nelson Mandela to power. He has worked across Africa and became a Reuters staff photographer in 1997. He received the Abdul Sharif award at both the 1997 and 2000 South African Fuji Press Photography Awards.

John Kolesidis
Born in Athens, Greece in 1973. John has worked as a news photographer since 1994.

Eduard Kornienko
Born in Stavropol, Russia in 1974. Worked for ITAR-TASS and other international media before joining Reuters in December 2003 as a freelancer. Eduard is currently a staff photographer of the Stavropol Pravda.

Dima Korotayev
Born in 1973. Dima has worked for EPA and AFP before joining Reuters in 1994. Assignments have taken him to Karabakh, Tbilisi, Abkhazia and Chechnya.

Viktor Korotayev
Born in Vakhtan, former USSR in 1951. Viktor became a photographer in 1974 for the TASS agency. He joined Reuters in 1989 during the Perestroika period. He covered the first and second coups in Moscow, Chechen wars, Bosnia and Kosovo crisis and events in Iraq and is now based in Moscow.

Reinhard Krause
Born in Essen, Germany in 1959. Reinhard joined Reuters as the Berlin Wall came down in 1989. He was made Chief Photographer for Israel and the Palestinian Territories in 2000. He is now Chief Photographer in China.

Adrees Latif
Born in Lahore, Pakistan in 1973. Adrees was a staff photographer at The Houston Post from 1993 to 1996. He started freelancing for Reuters in 1996 in Houston, Texas and from 2001 till 2003 in Los Angeles, California. Adrees is now Thailand Senior Photographer, based in Bangkok.

Philippe Laurenson
Born in Perpignan, France in 1965. Philippe has been freelancing for Reuters for ten years.

Francois Lenoir
Born in Brussels, Belgium in 1973. Francois has worked for two national agencies, Way Press and Isopress, before joining Reuters as a freelancer in March 2000.

Dylan Martinez
Born in Barcelona, Spain in 1969. Dylan began freelancing for Reuters in 1990 and has worked in Vietnam and London before becoming Italy Chief Photographer in 2001. He is now based in London.

Jeff J Mitchell
Born in Scotland in 1970. Jeff joined Reuters in 1996, based in Edinburgh. He has won numerous awards including Photographer of the Year at the UK Picture Editors' Awards for the second time in 2005.

Bazuki Muhammad
Born in Kuala Lumpur, Malaysia in 1965. Based in Kuala Lumpur, shooting politics, features, sports, and economics for Reuters since 1998. Bazuki won first prize in the Nature category at Malaysia's tourist board competition in 2005.

Gustau Nacarino
Born in 1949. Gustau began freelancing for Reuters in 1992. He also teaches Reportage and News Photography at the Polytechnic University of Catalonia near Barcelona.

Jacky Naegelen
Born in Colmar, France in 1956. Jacky studied photography in Paris. He worked as a freelance photographer in eastern France and joined Reuters in 1985. Jacky won the Sports category at Images Jazz in 2005.

Stoyan Nenov
Born in Sofia, Bulgaria in 1981. Stoyan joined Reuters in 2003 after working for several newspapers.

Jagadeesh Nv
Born in Bangalore, India in 1969. Jagadeesh has worked for Reuters since 2003.

Kai Pfaffenbach
Born in Hanau, Germany in 1970. Kai began working for Reuters as a freelance photographer in 1996 before becoming a staff photographer in 2001. He is currently based in Frankfurt.

Vladimir Pirogov
Born in Barabinsk, Novosibirsk in 1958. Vladimir has worked for Reuters since 2002.

Oleg Popov
Born in Sofia, Bulgaria in 1956. Oleg joined Reuters in 1990 as Chief Photographer in Bulgaria and has covered the wars in Slovenia, Croatia and Bosnia, Chechnya and Kosovo. He is currently Chief Photographer in Israel.

Marcelo del Pozo
Born in Seville, Spain in 1970. Based in Seville, he has covered a variety of events including the World Athletics Championships in 1999, the 2002 European Union summit, the San Fermin Bull Run in Pamplona in 2003 and the World Swimming Championships in Barcelona in 2003.

Wolfgang Rattay
Born in Bad Ems, Germany in 1960. Wolfgang worked for the Associated Press until he joined Reuters in 1985. In 1996 he was appointed Germany Chief Photographer. He is now Senior Photographer, with responsibility for editing, organising and shooting major assignments in Europe.

Mohsin Raza
Born in Lahore, Pakistan in 1965. Mohsin worked as a sports photographer at the daily Frontier Post Lahore before joining Reuters in 1988.

Jose Manuel Ribeiro
Born in Lisbon, Portugal in 1960. Jose began working as a freelance newspaper photographer and at the Portuguese agency LUSA in 1987. He joined Reuters in 1996.

Jessica Rinaldi
Born in Waterbury, Connecticut in 1979. Jessica became a freelance photographer for Reuters in 2003, photographing news and sports in the Boston area including the 2004 World Series, New Hampshire Primaries and the 2004 United States Presidential election.

Rickey Rogers
Born in Long Island, New York in 1957. Rickey moved to Bolivia in 1986 and began freelancing for Reuters and a variety of U.S. and European media, opening Bolivia's first national photo agency in 1994. He was hired by Reuters as Chief Photographer of southern Latin America in 1997 before moving to Brazil as Latin America Chief Photographer in 2003.

Max Rossi
Born in Rome, Italy in 1965. From 1996 to 2002, Max worked for Famiglia Cristiana magazine, covering national and international stories. Max joined Reuters in 2003 and is now a staff photographer.

Damir Sagolj
Born in Sarajevo in 1971. Damir worked with the Paris based Sipa press photo agency as their Bosnia photographer before joining Reuters as a staff photographer in 1997. He has covered major events in the Balkans, Middle East and Americas.

Akram Saleh
Born in Iraq in 1973. Akram began working for local newspapers before joining the Iraqi News Agency for 7 years. He started working exclusively for Reuters in 2003. Akram won first prize in Baghdad's International fair (2000-2001).

Suhaib Salem
Born in Gaza. Suhaib joined Reuters in 1997 as a freelancer and later as a full time staff photographer. He has covered major news stories in Iraq, Saudi Arabia, Jordan, Iran, United Arab Emirates, and the 2002 World Cup. In 2001, he won third place in the Spot News category at the World Press Photo contest and an Arab Journalist award.

Mohammad Shahidullah

Born in Dhaka in 1950. Mohammad started his career as a photographer at the Kishan Dhaka daily newspaper in 1979. He has worked as a Reuters freelance photographer for over 10 years.

Jayanta Shaw

Born in Calcutta, India in 1966. Jayanta started his career in 1986 as a freelance photographer in Calcutta. He then joined the Bengali daily newspaper Bartaman before joining Reuters in 1988.

Radu Sigheti

Born in Bucharest, Romania in 1959. Radu began working for Reuters in 1990 and is currently Chief Photographer in Kenya.

Jorge Silva

Born in Mexico City in 1975. Jorge began working with Agence France-Presse in 1998 in Mexico. He joined Reuters in 2000 as a freelancer based in Guatemala City and became a full-time staff photographer in 2003.

Bob Strong

Born in the USA in 1952. Bob began working with UPI in 1979. He has covered conflicts in El Salvador, Nicaragua, Colombia and Haiti for Reuters. Bob has been based in Baghdad as Iraq Chief Photographer since 2004.

Chaiwat Subprasom

Born in Phitsanulok province north of Bangkok, Thailand in 1971. Chaiwat worked as a photographer at a local newspaper before joining Reuters in 2004.

You Sung-Ho

Born in Pusan, Korea in 1977. You joined Reuters as a freelancer in 2004.

Goran Tomasevic

Born in Belgrade in 1969. Goran began working as a photographer in 1991 for the daily newspaper, Politika, throughout the former Yugoslavia. He started working for Reuters as a freelance photographer in 1996 during the anti-Milosevic demonstrations. Tomasevic was based in Baghdad during the Iraq conflict and is now based in Jerusalem.

Mahfouz abu Turk

Born in Hebron in 1949. Mahfouz became a freelance photographer in 1989 working for AFP and AP. He joined Reuters in 1996.

Sergei Vasiliev

Born in Smorgon, Belarus in 1966. Sergei has worked as a photographer since 1991 in several local and central Belarussian newspapers.

Mark Wallheiser

Born in Louisville, Kentucky in 1954. Mark joined the Montgomery Advertiser and Alabama Journal in 1978 then the Tallahassee Democrat in 1981 where he has worked for the past 24 years. He is a past Florida News Photographer of the Year and was nominated for the Pulitzer Prize in 1989.

Darren Whiteside

Born in Toronto, Canada in 1965. Darren joined Reuters in 1995 and is currently based in Jakarta, Indonesia. He has worked in Somalia, Japan, Afghanistan and East Timor.

Philippe Wojazer

Born in Paris, France in 1959. Philippe joined Agence France-Presse in 1981 before joining Reuters in Paris in 1985.

Bobby Yip

Born in Hong Kong in 1962. Bobby started work as a local press photographer before joining Reuters in 1990, based in Hong Kong. He was the chairman of the Hong Kong Press Photographers' Association in 1994, 1999, 2003 and 2004.

Shamil Zhumatov

Born in Almaty, Kazakhstan in 1971. Shamil joined Reuters in 1994, covering Kazakhstan, Kyrgyztan, Tajikistan, Turkmenistan and Uzbekistan. He has also worked on the earthquakes in Afghanistan in 1998 and in Iran in 2004, as well as the conflict in Afghanistan during 2001-2002, and the annual Hajj pilgrimage and Iraq war in 2003.

Srdjan Zivulovic

Born in Koper, Slovenia in 1959. Srdjan studied photography before working for national newspaper Delo. He has run his own photo agency and has been working as a Reuters freelancer since 1991.

Pearson Education Limited

Edinburgh Gate
Harlow CM20 2JE
Tel: +44 (0)1279 623623
Fax: +44 (0)1279 431059
Website: www.pearsoned.co.uk

First published in Great Britain in 2005

ISBN 0 273 70631 4

British Library Cataloguing-in Publication Data
A catalogue record for this book is available from the British Library

10 9 8 7 6 5 4 3 2 1
09 08 07 06 05

Edited by Ayperi Ecer and Jassim Ahmad

With special thanks to Alexia Singh, Simon Newman, Catherine Benson,
Angela Kearney, Valerie Bezzina, Aldrina Thirunagaran, Dennis Yeo,
Leslie D'Souza, Kimitsu Yogachi, Louise Buckley, Susan Allsopp,
Victoria Simpson

Designed by SMITH

Printed and bound in Great Britain by Bath Press

The publisher's policy is to use paper manufactured from
sustainable forests.

The images in this book were taken in the course of news gathering
and/or journalistic activities for or by Reuters. None of the subjects
within any of the images sponsors or endorses the book in any way.